HUMAN FOSSILS

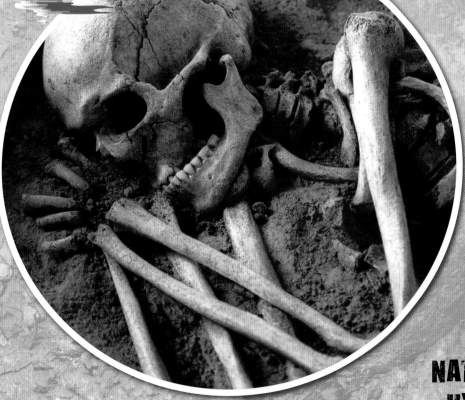

NATALIE
HYDE

Crabtree Publishing Company

www.crabtreebooks.com

IF THESE FOSSILS COULD TALK

Author
Natalie Hyde

Publishing plan research and development
Reagan Miller

Editor and indexer
Crystal Sikkens

Proofreader
Adrianna Morganelli

Design
Margaret Amy Salter

Photo research
Margaret Amy Salter, Crystal Sikkens

**Production coordinator
and prepress technician**
Samara Parent

Print coordinator
Margaret Amy Salter

Photographs
Bridgeman Art Library: © Wolfgang Neeb: page 23 (bottom);
   © Werner Forman Archive: page 25
Getty Images: © Ira Block: page 10; © Gamma-Rapho: page 22
Science Source: © Spencer Sutton: page 5; © John Reader:
   page 9 (top); © Javier Trueba / Madrid Scientific Films:
   page 11 (top); © Philippe Plailly: page 11 (bottom); © Javier
   Trueba / Madrid Scientific Films: page 13 (bottom); © John
   Reader: page 18
Thinkstock: pages 4, 28 (bottom left)
Wikimedia Commons: © Daniele Florio: page 3;
   © hairymuseummatt: page 8 (top); © John G. Murdoch:
   page 8 (bottom); © Peter Maas: page 9 (bottom);
   © Altaileopard: page 12; © Jonathan Cardy: page 13 (top);
   © Ryan Somma: page 14; : © Tobias Fluegel: page 15 (top);
   © Andrew: page 15 (bottom); © Tim Evanson: page 16
   (bottom); © James Gordon: page 17 (top); © Max Planck
   Institute for Evolutionary Anthropology: page 17 (bottom);
   © Sianto et al. 2012: page 19 (top); © Raveesh Vyas: page 19
   (bottom); © Anrie: page 26 (top); © John Cooke: page 26
   (bottom); © public domain: page 27 (top); © Rafał
   Chałgasiewicz: page 27 (bottom)
All other images by Shutterstock

Library and Archives Canada Cataloguing in Publication

Hyde, Natalie, 1963-, author
    Human fossils / Natalie Hyde.

(If these fossils could talk)
Includes index.
Issued in print and electronic formats.
ISBN 978-0-7787-1263-3 (bound).--ISBN 978-0-7787-1267-1
(pbk.).-- ISBN 978-1-4271-8957-8 (pdf).--ISBN 978-1-4271-8953-0
(html)

    1. Fossil hominids--Juvenile literature. I. Title.

GN282.H93 2013   j569.9   C2013-905235-6
                                        C2013-905236-4

Library of Congress Cataloging-in-Publication Data

CIP available at Library of Congress

Crabtree Publishing Company

www.crabtreebooks.com   1-800-387-7650

Printed in Canada/092013/BF20130815

**Published in Canada
Crabtree Publishing**
616 Welland Ave.
St. Catharines, Ontario
L2M 5V6

**Published in the United States
Crabtree Publishing**
PMB 59051
350 Fifth Avenue, 59th Floor
New York, New York 10118

**Published in the United Kingdom
Crabtree Publishing**
Maritime House
Basin Road North, Hove
BN41 1WR

**Published in Australia
Crabtree Publishing**
3 Charles Street
Coburg North
VIC 3058

CONTENTS

OUR HUMAN PAST

Fossils are like a time machine. By studying the preserved remains of our human ancestors, we can visit the past. Information about the lives and deaths of people who lived thousands of years ago is locked in their bones, teeth, and footprints.

OUR HISTORY

Paleoanthropologists are scientists who study **primitive** man by examining human fossils. They try to figure out how we evolved into the people we are today. Fossils from over 6,000 human **ancestors** have been discovered. Like a giant picture puzzle, paleoanthropologists work to put the pieces in order to uncover a picture of our **evolution**.

With each new fossil found, paleoanthropologists are sorting out who we are and how we came to be.

THE FAMILY TREE

One thing paleoanthropologists have learned is that there is not a straight line from early humans to modern ones. Our past is like a tree with many branches. With new discoveries being made every year, the human family tree is bigger and older than we ever imagined.

WHO ARE WE?

There were times in our history when two or three different species all lived at the same time, and even in the same place. Modern humans, called *Homo sapiens*, are the only surviving relative of that tree. The size and shape of our family tree is still being debated.

NOTEWORTHY NAMES

Meave Leakey and her husband found a partial skull in Kenya in 1999. Called the "flat-faced man," this fossil completely changed our understanding of early human ancestry. It indicated that during one time period, there existed more than one species of early human that could walk upright.

Many scientists believe humans evolved from apes. Apes have smaller brains and walk on all fours. Eventually, humans grew bigger brains and started walking upright. Scientists are still trying to find out why.

MADE IN MANY WAYS

When paleoanthropologists study human bones, they are looking for answers about our evolution. By examining the shape and size of bones and teeth, they can follow how early humans learned new skills or adapted **to changes in their environment.**

WALKING ON TWO FEET

Our ancestors used both their arms and legs to get around. An important step in human evolution was how and when early man learned to walk upright. Clues to this change are found in the knees. A wide area below the knee showed they could handle the stress of walking on two legs.

*Other clues to this change include a curved spine that could **absorb** shock and wider hip bones for easier movement.*

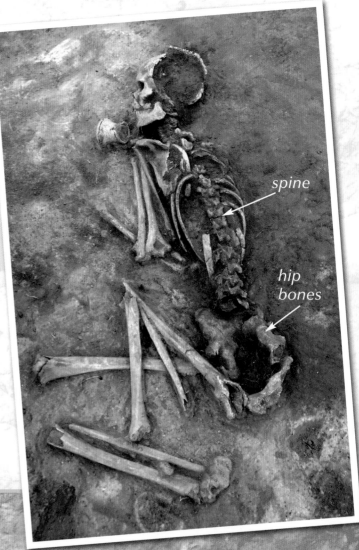

spine

hip bones

TOOTH STORY

New layers of enamel grow on teeth each year and scientists can read them to tell the age of a skeleton. This is important information for scientists. They can estimate how long people lived and also how fast they matured.

BIG BRAINS

After studying human skulls, paleoanthropologists were surprised to discover that new skills such as walking upright and making tools did not result in a big increase in brain size. The human brain did, however, make huge leaps in size during a time when humans spread around the globe and experienced new environments and climates.

How were early humans similar to apes?

Examining the size and shape of human skulls helps paleoanthropologists understand when and why our brains grew bigger.

FIRST FOSSILS

The first human fossils were skulls discovered in 1829 and 1848 in Engis, Belgium. No one was sure what to think of them. They were thicker than a modern human skull and had a large brow ridge over the eyes.

This photo shows a comparison of a modern human skull and a Neanderthal's.

Human

Neanderthal

THE FIRST HUMAN FOSSILS

These first fossils were not recognized as human skulls until another skull and various bones were discovered in 1856 in the Neander Valley in Germany. These early humans were named Neanderthals, after the Valley where the first recognized human skull was found.

NEW IDEAS

Charles Darwin suggested in his book, "Origin of the Species," that living things evolved over time. In his next work, Darwin put forward the idea that man shared an ancestor with apes. This idea was not accepted easily.

portrait of Charles Darwin

APE-MAN

A young scientist named Eugene Dubois read Darwin's work and wondered if more human fossils might be found in Africa. After four years, he found a skeleton in Java of something not quite human but not quite ape. It stood upright but had a much smaller brain than a modern human.

MORE BELIEVERS

After many more fossils of early humans were found in the 1900s, Darwin's idea that humans evolved was starting to be accepted. Today, more than 20 **hominid** species have been identified, helping scientists learn more about our ancestors.

(above) "Java man" was called Pithecanthropus erectus, *which means "upright ape-man," later named* Homo erectus. *Dubois created a model of what he believed Java man looked like.*

Java man was not a complete skeleton. Dubois found only a skullcap, a leg bone, and a few teeth.

Charles Darwin studied organisms in nature. The fossils he collected on his trip aboard the HMS *Beagle* led to his theories on how plants and animals came to be. His work, including the theory of "natural selection," is the reason he is called one of the most **influential** figures in human history.

TAKING A BITE OUT OF ANCIENT MAN

Fossil teeth are an excellent way of studying and comparing different species of ancient humans. It is one of the most common human fossils. Enamel is an extremely hard material and survives the fossilization process very well.

LINES OF GROWTH

As teeth grow they leave growth lines each day in their **crowns** and roots. This can help scientists figure out how old someone was when they died. Using this method, scientists learn how slowly or quickly different species of early humans matured.

TOOTH SHAPE

The shape of teeth help paleoanthropologists group early humans. One trait is the shape of the incisors, or front teeth. They compare how shovel-shaped the tooth is from one species to another. They also compare tooth size, shape, enamel thickness, and how the jaw moved.

The Neanderthal's teeth have a very obvious shovel shape.

DIET DIARY

Enamel does more than just give an age for the skeleton. It also absorbs some of the elements from the food the person ate. By examining the enamel of early human fossil teeth, paleoanthropologists can learn their diet.

wisdom tooth

GOOD TIMES, BAD TIMES

Fossil teeth can also tell scientists a lot about an individual and his or her environment. Diseased or misshapen teeth show that the person struggled with his or her health. Growth is slowed when an area experiences a shortage of food from lack of rain or natural disasters.

This 800,000-year-old jaw bone is from a child. The wisdom tooth that has not yet come through tells scientists the child died around 14 years old.

A person's diet can also be seen by the number of molars and incisors they have. Molars for chewing, point to a plant-based diet, while sharp incisors for tearing at flesh, suggests a diet including meat.

incisor

molar

FACT FILE

Scientists study fossil teeth by photographing them through microscopes to see tiny wear marks. Scientists also use dental picks, chemicals, and lasers to find the smallest details.

BONE YARD

To date, scientists have found thousands of human bone fossils. Larger, thicker bones such as skulls, leg bones, and pelvises usually survive fossilization better than small bones such as fingers. They are rare, but there have been a few intact skeletons found.

OLD TIMER

The oldest bone fossil is about seven million years old. It was found in Chad, Africa, and includes a small skull, pieces of a jaw, and some teeth. Some scientists wonder if this fossil marks the time when humans split from apes.

HOME SWEET HOME

The oldest bones from our own species, *Homo sapiens*, were found in Ethiopia, Africa. They are 160,000-year-old skulls of two adult males and a child. This proved that our ancestors evolved in Africa and then moved to other parts of the world.

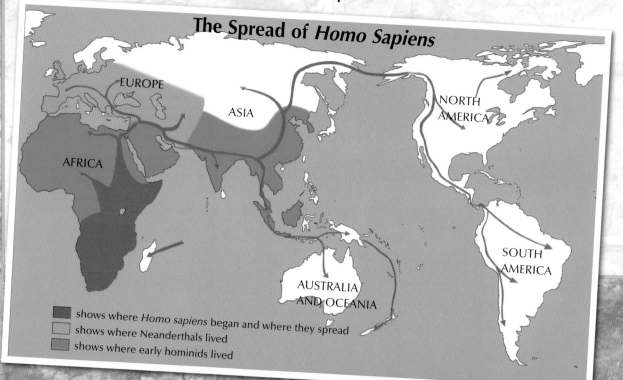

The Spread of *Homo Sapiens*

EUROPE

ASIA

NORTH AMERICA

AFRICA

SOUTH AMERICA

AUSTRALIA AND OCEANIA

shows where *Homo sapiens* began and where they spread
shows where Neanderthals lived
shows where early hominids lived

An important skull was found in the Broken Hill mine in Zambia, Africa. It is a very fine example of *Homo heidelbergensis*. Scientists believe this species is the most recent common ancestor to both Neanderthals and us, *Homo sapiens*.

CAN YOU HEAR ME?

The tiniest bones in the human body come from the ear. Fossils of three of these ear bones were found in South Africa and are about two million years old. That makes them some of the rarest human fossils ever found. One of the three bones looks very human-like and scientists wonder if modern patterns of hearing started around that time.

DINNER MENU

Just like teeth, bones absorb chemical elements from food and the environment. Researchers test the bones to discover what the individual ate and what plants and animals lived in the surrounding area.

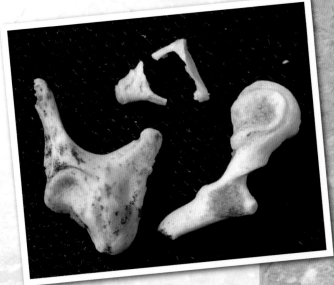

Ear bones from Homo heidelbergensis *dating back 400,000 years were found in a cave in Spain known as the "Pit of the Bones."*

LITTLE PEOPLE

On the remote Indonesian island of Flores, a team of archaeologists made an amazing discovery. In a cave they found skeletons of a species of hominid that was unlike anything they had seen before.

THE HOBBITS

They found a skull, pelvis, limbs, hands, and feet that belonged to a female that was only 3 feet (1 m) tall. Scientists named this new species *Homo floresiensis*, but they are nicknamed "hobbits" after the tiny people in J.R.R. Tolkien's book, *The Hobbit*.

SMALL BRAIN

The skull showed these early humans had a very small brain. The scientists also found tools near the remains. They were surprised that such a small brain was **complex** enough for making and using tools.

The shape of the Homo floresiensis *skull links this species closer to a human ancestor,* Homo erectus, *rather than modern humans.*

RECENT RELATIVES

The other amazing thing about these little hominids is that the fossils are not that old. They show that this species was living on Flores as recently as 17,000 years ago. Scientists believe that a volcano erupted in the area and caused this species to become extinct.

ARDI

One of the oldest skeletons ever found is nicknamed "Ardi." She lived about 4.4 million years ago in Ethiopia, Africa. Her bones were so fragile that they crumbled when touched, but they told scientists that she could walk on two feet as well as swing through the trees.

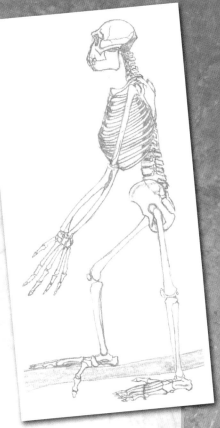

Ardi had a big toe that spread out from her foot, similar to apes, so she could easily grip branches.

LUCY

Lucy was the name given to the three-million-year-old skeleton of an early human-like ape found in Ethiopia. Its proper name is *Australopithecus afarensis*. Amazingly, over forty percent of her skeleton was found. Lucy is believed to have been 3 feet, 7 inches (1.1 m) tall.

Lucy had strong upper arms to help her climb trees. She also had leg bones that allowed her to walk upright.

? Why were scientists surprised that tools were found with the "hobbit" remains?

DISTANT COUSIN

Our closest extinct relatives are Neanderthals. Neanderthal fossils have been found in Europe and parts of Asia. The fossils showed many similarities as well as differences between us and our distant relatives.

Tools such as this flint axe head, show that Neanderthals were skilled at making tools.

WHAT DID THEY LOOK LIKE?

Fossils show that Neanderthals were shorter and stockier than *Homo sapiens* and probably stronger. They also had a thick brow over their eyes. Their brains were just as large as ours and sometimes larger.

Fossils show Neanderthals had large noses. Researchers are still trying to find out why this was.

JUST LIKE US?

Advanced tools were found near Neanderthal bones. Fireplaces used for cooking food, and the remains of shelters made of animal bones and skins were also nearby. Examination of their fossilized teeth showed that they not only ate meat, but also cooked plants as part of their diet.

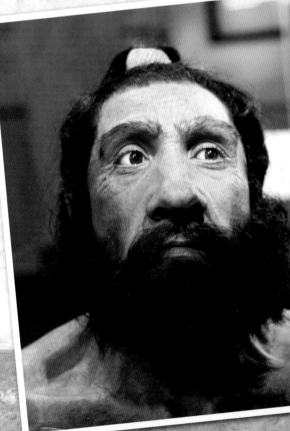

CARING COMMUNITY

The skull of a skeleton named "Shanidar 1" showed he had a crushing blow to his head when he was young. The hit damaged the part of his brain that controlled the right side of his body. This caused the bone of his right arm to be smaller and weaker than the left. His right leg was also affected so that he probably limped. But researchers saw that this did not cause his death. In fact, he lived to be about 40 years old. This told scientists that others must have cared for him.

Shanidar 1 skull

How are Neanderthals similar to *Homo sapiens*? How are they different?

CLOSER THAN YOU THINK

Scientists are trying to map the DNA of Neanderthals. They are excited to learn more about our distant cousins. They have found evidence that Neanderthals and *Homo sapiens* not only lived at the same time, but may have had babies together. New **genetic** studies show that all non-Africans are part Neanderthal.

Scientists remove Neanderthal's DNA from their bone fossils.

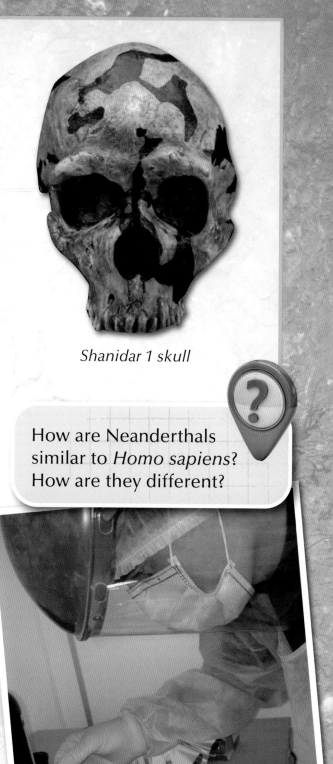

LEFT BEHIND

Trace fossils are records of an organism's activity. Human trace fossils include coprolites, or fossilized poop, and footprints and handprints.

PRINTS IN ASH

The oldest human fossil footprints were found in northern Tanzania. These 3.6-million-year-old footprints were made by two adults and possibly a child that walked in wet volcanic ash. The prints show the humans were walking on two feet. The **trackway** is nearly 88 feet (27 m) long and shows about 70 footprints.

To the right of the Tanzania human footprints are prints from a hipparion, an extinct three-toed horse.

WHO GOES THERE?

Human footprints were also found in southern Italy. They are about 325,000 years old and show that three humans walked down a slope covered in ash after a volcanic eruption. Along the trackway are a few handprints as well, where they must have used their hands to steady themselves on the difficult trip down.

FOSSIL POOP

Coprolites are a great source of information for scientists. Pollen found inside these rocks show researchers what kinds of plants our ancestors ate. They can also show what kinds of **bacteria** were present thousands of years ago and whether or not the individual might have been ill.

Human coprolites are dry, non-smelly, and made of stone, so studying them isn't as disgusting as you might think.

Some of the cave paintings in the Bhimbetka rock shelters, in India, are around 30,000 years old.

FACT FILE

Some scientists also consider tools, building foundations, wall art, carvings, and graves trace fossils because they show ancient human activity. They give paleoanthropologists a look into the behavior, habits, and customs of early humans.

CAST AND MOLD FOSSILS

Sometimes the bones of an individual do not fossilize, but the shape of their body can leave an impression. This type of fossil is called a mold. If material fills the mold, it will take the shape of what was once there. This is called a cast.

BURIED IN ASH

Molds and casts of humans are rare, but an unexpected event almost 2,000 years ago left archaeologists with an amazing collection of human molds. In 79 AD, Mount Vesuvius, in Italy, erupted sending ash and rocks down upon the towns of Pompeii and Herculaneum. It happened so quickly that people were not able to escape. They were buried alive.

The volcanic ash from Mount Vesuvius left a picture of what the cities looked like the day they were buried thousands of years ago.

*The body casts from Pompeii give information about what the people were doing when they died and give **insights** into early Roman life.*

BODY CASTS

Giuseppe Fiorelli, an Italian archaeologist, helped to preserve the lost city of Pompeii. He realized that the ash had hardened before the bodies decayed, leaving a mold. He pumped plaster into the holes to make a cast of the shape of the bodies. Over 30 body casts have been made.

HERCULANEUM

Only a few miles away from Pompeii was Herculaneum. While Pompeii was covered under 82 feet (25 m) of ash, Herculaneum was buried under hot volcanic material that instantly killed anyone in its path, but preserved their bones. These remains gave researchers the real story of what happened and important information about the workings of volcanic eruptions.

?

What is the difference between a mold and a cast fossil?

FROZEN IN TIME

Flash freezing is a remarkable way to preserve a body. As well as bones and teeth, flesh, hair, nails, and clothing are all preserved when they are frozen. This is what happened to a man 5,300 years ago when he took a wrong step on a glacier.

ICEMAN

The iceman is known as Ötzi because he was found in the Ötztal Alps. Ötzi's axe blade, tooth enamel, and pollen in his stomach revealed that he probably lived in the Vinschgau Valley in the Alps.

Ötzi was found by two tourists walking along a mountain path. They did not know how old he was or how important he would become.

ÖTZI'S LAST DAYS

Paleoanthropologists learned a lot from having soft tissue and **artifacts** preserved with the body. From lines on his fingernails they knew he had been sick two weeks before he died. They found chemicals in his hair that suggested he **smelted** copper for a living. They also found tattoos on his back that they think might have been to treat pain.

ICY LEGACY

Ötzi has given scientists valuable information about the past. Because of how much of the body was preserved, researchers have studied how diseases began and even how wheat has evolved. They are also getting information on climate change and how it affects plants and animals.

FACT FILE Because of climate change glaciers are melting and exposing more artifacts and fossils. In the Yukon in Canada researchers found a small 4,300-year-old dart with **sinew** and a bit of feather on it. These materials normally decompose but were preserved in the frozen ice patches.

Canada's Yukon Territory

By examining his stomach, researchers found that Ötzi's last meal was goat and deer meat and herb bread.

23

BOGGED DOWN

A bog is a swampy piece of ground that is spongy and wet. It is a place where layers of dead plants create peat and where blueberries and cranberries grow. It is also a great place to preserve a body.

BOG BODIES

Unlike bodies that are buried in the ground and decompose, bodies in bogs do not rot. The water is so **acidic** that bodies that end up in a bog often still have their skin, organs, hair, and clothing. Most bog bodies are from the Iron Age, about 3,000 years ago. Many of them seem to have been a type of human sacrifice. Scientists found items on the bodies that look like offerings to the gods, such as neck-rings and ankle-rings.

The acid in bog water comes from decaying plants.

CAPITAL PUNISHMENT

Other bog bodies have evidence that points to the idea that they were criminals being punished. The preserved skin of these bodies show signs of being stabbed, beaten, or strangled. The Tollund Man from Denmark was found with the rope still around his neck from his hanging.

FACT FILE

Preserving bog bodies once they are out of the bog water is a tricky thing. Scientists tried smoking the body of the Tollund Man to prevent decaying. This worked but it made the body dry out and shrink.

For the Tollund Man's head they replaced the bog water in the cells with bees wax.

SWAMPY CEMETERY

Bog bodies have also been found in a muck pond in Florida. The bodies of 168 people were found buried in peat at the bottom of the pond. The peat preserved the brains inside their skulls and allowed scientists to study them. The bodies were wrapped in fabrics and had **grave goods** with them, telling scientists that this was the site of a burial ground of people who died of natural causes.

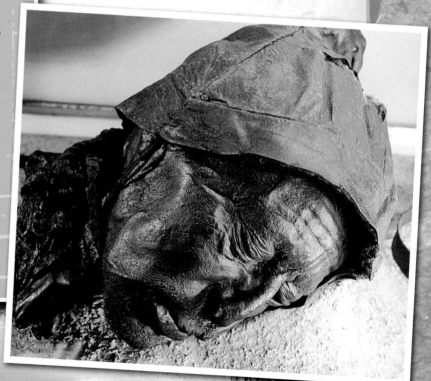

FAKES AND FALSEHOODS

There is still a lot of debate over the origins of man. Sometimes people create false artifacts or fossils. These hoaxes can go on for many years and waste valuable time for scientists.

piltdown skull

THE PILTDOWN MAN

In 1912, two **amateur** archaeologists announced to the world that they had found the "missing link" between man and apes. They had found an ancient human-like skull in Piltdown, England. The skull showed a large brain, like humans, but a jaw like an ape with human-looking teeth.

HOAX!

Forty years later scientists used new technology to examine the skull and found that the skull and jaw came from two different species—a human and an orangutan. It was a hoax.

Scientists were suspicious when more fossils were found that did not look anything like the Piltdown Man.

THE CARDIFF GIANT

The Cardiff Giant was another famous hoax. Two men digging a well in Cardiff, New York, found a strange stone. It was solid rock and the shape of a 10-foot, 5-inch (3.2 m) tall man. He was proof that giants once existed. In the end it was revealed as a hoax.

GIANT

In 1866, miners in California found a human skull in a mine. It was found below a layer of lava putting its age at the same time as the dinosaurs. Scientists studied the skull and found that it was a modern skull. Eventually some miners who had a grudge against the mine owner admitted that the skull came from a nearby cemetery and it was a practical joke.

(above) The Cardiff Giant was created by a man named George Hull who paid a stonecutter to carve a block of **gypsum** to look like a giant man.

FACT FILE

The Crystal skulls are human-shaped skulls made out of quartz crystal. They were said to be from ancient Aztec or Mayan civilizations. Research showed that they were carved using jeweler's equipment from the 1800s.

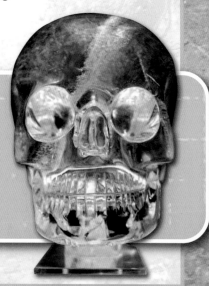

GIVE ME A HAND!

Make a plaster cast of your own hand. Another person will need to help you when doing this activity.
You will need:

plaster of paris

mixing bowl

hammer and chisel

dish soap

water

newspaper

petroleum jelly

wax paper

wooden spoon

baking sheet

1. Cover your work area with newspaper. Mix the plaster in the mixing bowl.

2. Place a 12-inch (30 cm) square of wax paper on the newspaper.

3. Rub petroleum jelly all over the hand that you are going to cast. Place that hand in the center of the waxed paper and press your hand down firmly.

4. Have another person scoop the plaster from the bowl and place it over your hand. Continue until the plaster is about 1 inch (2.5 cm) thick. Have your helper wash out the rest of the plaster and clean the bowl. Hold your hand still while the plaster hardens—about 10 to 15 minutes.

5. When the plaster begins to feel warm, it is time to remove your hand. Wiggle your fingers very carefully and slowly pull your hand from the mold. If for some reason the plaster breaks, do not worry! Simply glue the pieces in place after the mold is turned over.

6. Turn the completed mold over. Rub a layer of dishwashing soap over the impression of your hand.

7. Pour about 0.5 inches (1 cm) of water in the baking sheet. Sit the plaster hand mold in the water so the hand **indentation** is up. Allow the mold to soak for five minutes. The plaster must be covered in water so the new mold of your hand will pop out easily.

8. Remove the mold from the water and place it on the wax paper. Mix a second batch of plaster.

9. Carefully spoon the mixed plaster in the hand indentation until it is about 1 inch (2.5 cm) above the surface of the mold. This is the base for the hand. Allow the plaster to dry for one hour.

10. Turn the mold over. Use a chisel and hammer to break away the plaster mold.

GLOSSARY

absorb Soak up

acidic Containing chemicals that dissolve metals

adapted Become adjusted to new conditions

amateur Not professional

ancestors Early humans from whom we evolved or are related to

artifacts Ancient objects made by a human being

bacteria One-celled organisms

complex Complicated; made of many different parts

crowns The top part of a tooth covered by enamel

evolution The slow development from one thing to another

genetic Relating to genes or heredity

glacier A slow-moving river of ice down a mountain

grave goods Items buried with a body

gypsum A white or grey mineral

hominid The family of primates that includes humans

indentation A groove in a surface

influential Powerful and important

insights Deep understanding

intact In one piece; not damaged

peat A type of soil made from decayed plants

primitive An early stage in development

sinew A thread of tissue that connects a muscle to a bone

smelted To extract metals by heating and melting

trackway Two or more footprints showing a pattern of movement

LEARNING MORE

FURTHER READING:

Aronson, Marc. *The Skull in the Rock: How a Scientist, a Boy, and Google Earth Opened a New Window on Human Origins.* National Geographic Children's Books, 2012.

Connors, Kathleen. *Human Fossils*. Gareth Stevens Publishing, 2012.

Gamlin, Linda. *Evolution*. DK Children, 2009.

Loxton, Daniel. *Evolution: How We and All Living Things Came to Be.* Kids Can Press, 2010.

Sloan, Christopher. *The Human Story: Our Evolution from Prehistoric Ancestors to Today*. National Geographic Children's Books, 2004.

WEBSITES:

The Smithsonian National Museum of Natural History: What does it mean to be human?
http://humanorigins.si.edu/evidence/human-fossils

Fact Monster on human evolution:
www.factmonster.com/ipka/A0932663.html

Prehistoric humans from Kids Past:
www.kidspast.com/world-history/0001-prehistoric-humans.php

Early humans for kids:
http://earlyhumans.mrdonn.org

INDEX